Spotlight on
ANCIENT CIVILIZATIONS
ROME

Ancient Roman GEOGRAPHY

Amelie von Zumbusch

Published in 2014 by The Rosen Publishing Group, Inc.
29 East 21st Street, New York, NY 10010

First Edition

Book Design: Kate Vlachos
Layout Design: Andrew Povolny

Photo Credits: Cover Andrea Thompson Photography/Photolibrary/Getty Images; p. 4 Dorling Kindersley RF/Thinkstock; pp. 5, 20 iStockphoto/Thinkstock; p. 6 Natalia Barsukova/Shutterstock.com; p. 7 DEA/G. Nimatallah/De Agostini Picture Library/Getty Images; p. 8 Mike Randolph/Radius Images/Getty Images; p. 9 Andrew Povolny; p. 10 Roman/The Bridgeman Art Library/Getty Images; p. 11 (Top) DEA/A. Dagli Orti/De Agostini Picture Library/Getty Images; p. 11 (Bottom) DEA/J. E. Bulloz/De Agostini Picture Library/Getty Images; p. 12 Jorg Greuel/Photodisc/Getty Images; p. 13 De Agostini Picture Libary/Getty Images; p. 15 Rodger Eritja/Photolibrary/Getty Images; p. 16 Alex Havret/Dorling Kindersley/Getty Images; p. 17 Jason Friend/Photolibrary/Getty Images; p. 19 David Epperson/Digital Vision/Getty Images; p. 20 Lenar Musin/Shutterstock.com; p. 21 Peter Barritt/Robert Harding World Imagery/Getty Images.

Library of Congress Cataloging-in-Publication Data

Zumbusch, Amelie von.
Ancient Roman geography / by Amelie von Zumbusch. — First edition.
pages cm. — (Spotlight on ancient civilizations: Rome)
Includes index.
ISBN 978-1-4777-0779-1 (library binding) — ISBN 978-1-4777-0891-0 (pbk.) — ISBN 978-1-4777-0892-7 (6-pack)
1. Geography—Rome—History—Juvenile literature. 2. Geography, Ancient—Juvenile literature. 3. Rome—Civilization—Juvenile literature. 4. Civilization, Ancient—Juvenile literature. I. Title.
G86.Z86 2014
913.7—dc23

2013003708

Manufactured in the United States of America

CPSIA Compliance Information: Batch #S13PK2: For Further Information contact Rosen Publishing, New York, New York at 1-800-237-9932

CONTENTS

From City to Empire

Today, Rome is a busy city in Italy. Historians believe it grew out of settlements along the Tiber River that date back to the eighth century BC. The settlers were Latins, a people who lived in central Italy.

Map of the Roman Empire in AD 117

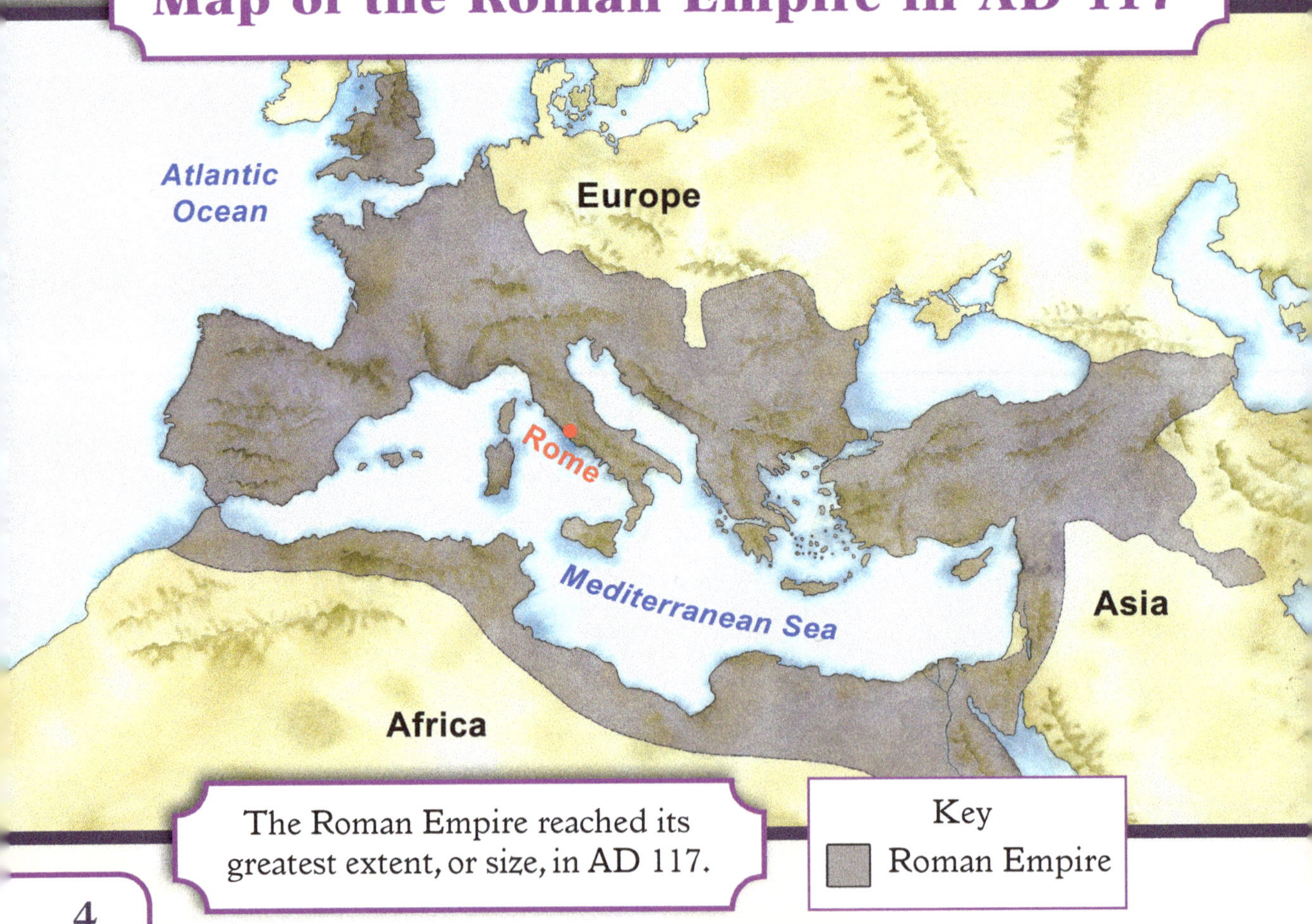

The Roman Empire reached its greatest extent, or size, in AD 117.

Traces of the Romans can be found across the lands they ruled. These are the ruins of the Roman city of Volubilis, in what is now Morocco.

Rome's power grew quickly. First, the Romans **conquered** other Latin settlements. Then they conquered other peoples in central Italy, such as the Etruscans and the Sabines. The Greek settlements of southern Italy fell to the Romans next. **Civilizations** around the Mediterranean Sea followed. At its height, Rome ruled a huge empire that stretched from Britain and Morocco in the west to Iraq in the east.

The Mediterranean Sea

Rome sits about halfway down the Italian **peninsula**. A peninsula is land that has water on three sides. The water surrounding Italy is the Mediterranean Sea. An arm of the Mediterranean called the Adriatic Sea lies east of Italy. The part of the Mediterranean west of Italy is the Tyrrhenian Sea.

This is the Mediterranean Sea. The Romans called it *mare nostrum*. This means "our sea" in Latin.

The Roman ship in this carving is being powered by oarsmen. These are people who row with big oars.

Rome is about 15 miles (24 km) inland from the coast. However, boats could reach it easily by going up the Tiber. Some of these boats were the trading ships that helped Rome grow rich. There were also ships that carried Roman soldiers off to conquer new lands.

On the Banks of the Tiber

Rome sits on the banks of Italy's second-longest river, the Tiber. It flows 252 miles (406 km), from Monte Fumaiolo in the Apennine Mountains to the Tyrrhenian Sea. The land Rome was built on was hilly and marshy. In fact, Rome is famous for its seven hills. At first the Romans lived on the hills. Later, they drained the marshes that lay in between.

This is how the Tiber River looks as it flows through Rome today. It is also known by its Italian name, the *Tevere*.

Map of Rome Around 350 BC

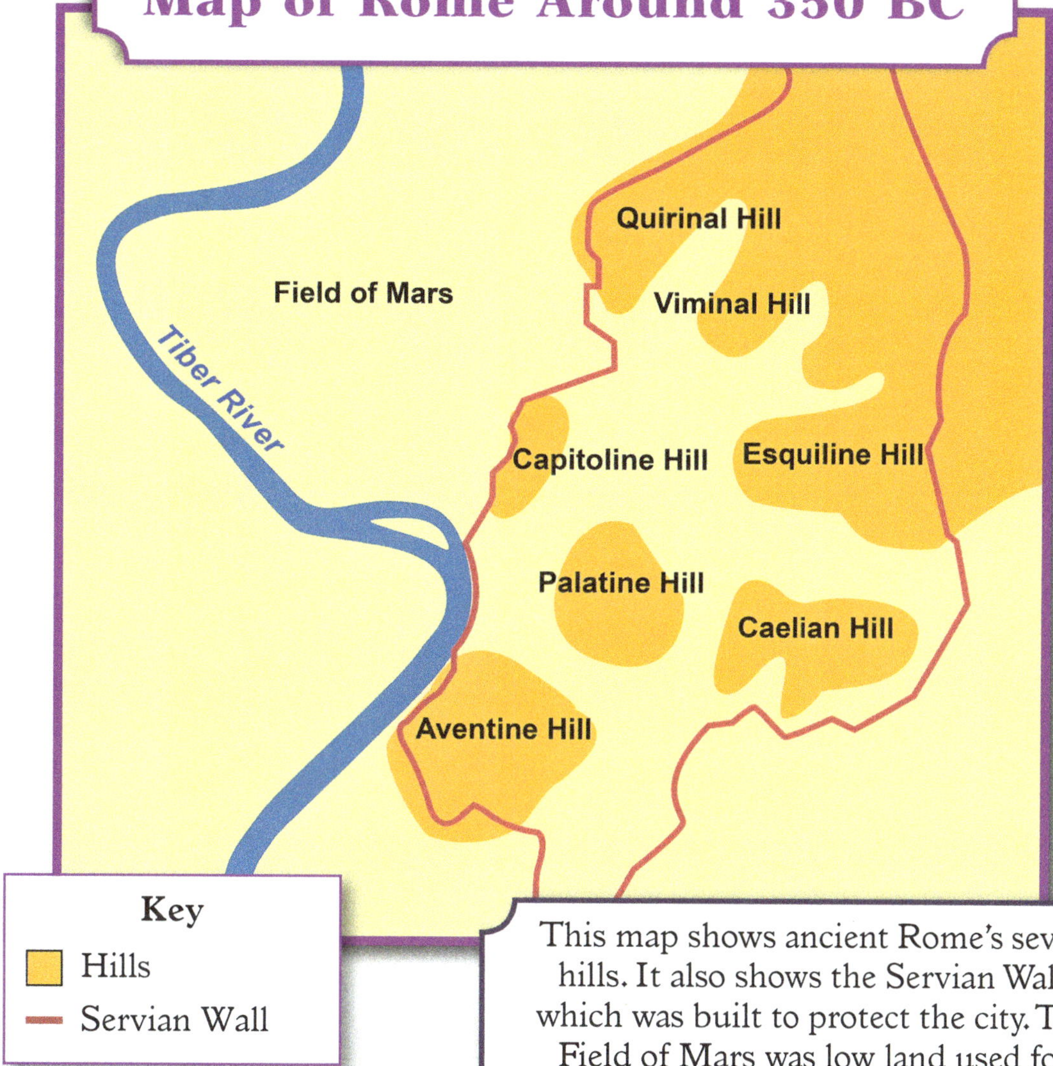

This map shows ancient Rome's seven hills. It also shows the Servian Wall, which was built to protect the city. The Field of Mars was low land used for military training and grazing animals.

The area around Rome is part of a big **plain**, known as Latium. It has a pleasant **climate**, with hot summers and mild winters. It gets a fair amount of rain, though it is drier in the summer.

Rich Land for Farming

Mountains cover much of Italy, but there is also plenty of **fertile** land. The fertile soil in Latium was good for growing crops. The Romans developed the Po River valley, in northern Italy, into the peninsula's richest area for farming.

Rome's pleasant climate let the Romans grow gardens with fruit trees, like the one in this Roman wall painting.

This carving shows a Roman mill for grinding wheat into flour. The donkey turns the top of the mill. The person guides the animal.

Most of the people living under Roman rule made their living by farming. The main crop was wheat. Olives and grapes were also key crops. At first, the Romans relied on wheat that was grown in Italy. Later, they **imported** wheat from other parts of their empire, such as Egypt. By that point, most crops were grown on huge farms called *latifundia*.

In this image, people are harvesting olives. The Romans used olives to make olive oil. They used the oil in cooking and to burn in lamps.

Natural Defenses

While Italy's fertile soil supplied the Romans with food, other landscape features were natural defenses. Early on, Rome's marshy, hilly location was hard to attack. The Mediterranean separated Rome from some enemies. The Apennine Mountains, which run down Italy's center, made it harder to attack from the north. The Alps, which are even higher and harder to cross, separate Italy from the rest of Europe.

The Alps cover about 80,000 square miles (207,199 sq km). They are easier to cross in the summer than in the winter.

To this day, the ancient Romans are remembered for their powerful, organized army. Roman soldiers, like those in this carving, were well trained.

These natural defenses did not always work. A people called the Gauls **sacked** Rome around 390 BC. Hannibal, a general from Rome's enemy Carthage, crossed the Alps in 218. To defend itself, Rome developed a powerful army.

Resources for Building

The Romans used many **natural resources** in building. They made bricks out of clay. They also made roof tiles from clay, sometimes mixing it with sand or straw. In Rome, many buildings used the **volcanic** rock tufa, which is common in that area. The rock alabaster was cut into thin sheets for windows.

The Romans are known for their long-lasting concrete. To make it, they baked limestone in big ovens until it turned powdery. They mixed that with water. They then added sand or volcanic ash. Volcanic ash made for the strongest concrete. Ash called *pozzolana* from Italy's Campania region was especially good.

A quarry is a place where rock is cut out of the ground. Rock from Spain's El Médol quarry, seen here, was used to build the nearby Roman city of Tarraco.

Roman Settlements

The city of Rome always remained at the center of Roman civilization, but there were other Roman towns and cities spread across the empire. Some were places that the Romans conquered and then remade in Rome's image. The Romans also founded towns. Some of these were places for retired Roman soldiers to live.

These are the ruins of a Roman villa, or country house, in what is now Germany. The Romans built villas in many provinces, or areas that they ruled.

Hadrian's Wall stretches across Great Britain from the Irish Sea to the North Sea. At the time it was built, it marked the limits of the Roman Empire.

Roman towns had a forum. This was a market and central gathering place. There was a town hall and law court, called a basilica. Most had public baths, where people could both meet with friends and get clean. Many cities were laid out in a grid pattern. City walls surrounded some cities.

Roman Roads

Roman towns were connected to Rome itself by means of a network of roads. These roads covered a total of 50,000 miles (80,467 km). Most of the roads were built by the Roman **legions**. These were divisions of the Roman army. The roads made it possible for the legions to move around the empire quickly.

To this day, Roman roads are famous for being straight and long-lasting. They were generally made of carefully cut stones, with two layers of sand and gravel underneath. They sloped down at the sides so that rainwater would run off them into ditches dug along their sides.

This is the Via Appia, or Appian Way. It was the first big Roman road. It was also among the most important. The Romans started building it in 312 BC.

Amazing Aqueducts

The early Romans got water for drinking and cooking from the Tiber or nearby springs. However, these became polluted, and the city needed a new source of water. The Romans built aqueducts to bring water from far-off springs and lakes to Rome.

When crossing big valleys, aqueducts ran over bridges made up of a series of arches. This Roman aqueduct bridge is in Spain.

Roman cities had many public drinking fountains. This one is in the Roman town of Pompeii, in Italy.

Water flows downhill, so the aqueducts tilted down at a slight angle. Water ran through covered channels, which ran on the ground, underground, and over bridges. By the third century AD, 11 aqueducts supplied Rome with water. It flowed through lead pipes to public baths, toilets, and fountains. The Romans also built aqueducts in nearly 200 other cities.

The Perfect Location

Ancient Rome's success had a lot to do with **geography**. Rome's land, water, and weather offered many advantages. The Romans picked a spot where the climate and rich soil were great for farming. The Tiber gave them easy access to the Mediterranean and helped stop attacks from the north.

Rome's central location in Italy made it the perfect place from which to conquer the rest of the peninsula. Once Rome ruled Italy, it was in a great position to conquer the western Mediterranean and beyond!

These are the ruins of Roman villas in Carthage. This North African city was an enemy of Rome. The Romans destroyed Carthage in 146 BC, but later rebuilt the city.

GLOSSARY

civilizations (sih-vih-lih-ZAY-shunz) People living in certain ways.

conquered (KON-kerd) Overcame something.

climate (KLY-mut) The kind of weather a certain place has.

fertile (FER-tul) Good for making and growing things.

geography (jee-AH-gruh-fee) The natural features of a place.

imported (im-PORT-ed) Brought in from another country for sale or use.

legions (LEE-jenz) Large military forces.

natural resources (NA-chuh-rul REE-sors-ez) Things in nature that can be used by people.

peninsula (peh-NIN-suh-luh) An area of land surrounded by water on three sides.

plain (PLAYN) An area of mostly flat land that has few or no trees.

sacked (SAKD) Destroyed.

volcanic (vol-KA-nik) Made by or having to do with volcanoes.

INDEX

WEBSITES

Due to the changing nature of Internet links, PowerKids Press has developed an online list of websites related to the subject of this book. This site is updated regularly. Please use this link to access the list:
www.powerkidslinks.com/sacr/geo/